Contents

Cover design by S.Y Lee-Wan
Layout by S.Y Lee-Wan
Editorial by Cory Lakatos
General Editor by Greg Smith
Publishing Consulting by Jen Hayes

ISBN: 978-1-7331346-0-6

Dedication

Jenny, Ben, Ana, Mia, and Aubrey—
Your love and support is priceless!

My Mom and Dad—
Always an encouraging voice and a patient presence.
I am grateful for and love both of you.

The Shifting Gears Leadership Team—
Just being around you makes me redefine "my best" often.

Phil, Steve, Trent, and Chase—
When I feel like a moody author, you just call me friend. Thanks.

In complexity, cause and effect are not predictable. Other people act in ways that don't make sense to us. Many interrelated factors affect what is emerging, and some things in the system affect others in ways impossible to predict. The harder we drive for results, the more the unanticipated side effects tend to multiply.

In these kinds of environments, the usual ways of leading are often ineffective, even counterproductive. It can be liberating to recognize that we've been spending too much energy in approaches that actually don't work.

What if leading could in fact be both easier and more successful?

To scaffold new actions in our own complex leadership context, the condition of presence is foundational. Presence is an internal state: the awareness of immediacy, stillness, inclusive awareness and possibility. This state enables us to sense the world as it actually is and to sense ourselves as we actually are. A rigorous embrace of reality leads to clarity, resilience and results that matter.

Presence-Based Leadership: Complexity Practices for Clarity, Resilience, and Results That Matter

Doug Silsbee

It seemed only appropriate to start this edition with a quote from a coaching mentor I was so blessed to work with when I first started my practice. Doug taught me about presence and the internal work we must all do as leaders in order to be more effective and resilient in an ever-changing world. This is an excerpt from Doug's last book that he published before his death in 2018. I treasure it, and thank Doug for all his wisdom that continues to guide and inspire me.

Foreword to this 2019 Version

Maya Angelou once said, "A bird doesn't sing because it has an answer, it sings because it has a song." I wrote this book around my passion for *maximizing growth and minimizing pain, helping people move to and past the tipping point of success.* For me, it was more of a song than a specific answer, and yet I offered actions for leaders that resonated with the song I shared. In the years since this was published I became more convinced of two things. First, almost all leaders care deeply for their people but get too busy to show it. And second, truly listening to someone else is the most important skill of a leader.

During the process of looking forward to my next book I looked back at this book and the word that I heard myself using most often in it was "honest." It jumped out at me, and as I thought about the ultimate goal of a people-centered leader, I realized it was an honest culture.

In working with growth-minded entrepreneurial leadership teams as an EOS Implementer™, I have witnessed the power of honesty, how it helps teams get to the right solution and how it galvanizes relationships when it is coupled with agape love. I have also seeing how it erodes relationships and teams when we begin measuring honesty in percentages or degrees, either in how much we share it or how we receive it. Seeing my words in a different way led me to what I am calling the Honest Culture Journey™. I will explain it more at the end and in my new book to be released later this year.

I will leave you with one lens to bring along with you as you read this book: be honest. I did not change any words, but at the end of each chapter I provided a simple tool for you to practice honesty with yourself, because that's where it starts.

Welcome to the Honest Culture Journey™!

Introduction

Way back in the seventeenth century, John Donne said that, "No man is an island, entire of itself." That seems especially important to remember in the workplace of our twenty-first-century value economy. Our culture, technology, supply chains, distribution channels, and communications networks all depend on teamwork: complex collaboration, pooled knowledge, and leveraged value. What was true in the Elizabethan England of John Donne is even more true in our globalized marketplace. Far from being replaceable cogs in a machine, we are contributing nodes in a distributed network. When we work together in the right ways, the whole becomes greater than the sum of the parts. Therefore, "plays well with others" is not just a category on a child's report card; it's an essential skill for a successful career in today's complicated and competitive organizations.

How can we learn to "work well with others?" If you're reading this, then you probably already care about and have some competence in collaboration, so you're concerned with improvement. How can you work better with others? How can the team you lead work better together and with the teams around it? How can you encourage and develop people who work well with others, and how can you help them multiply those traits in others whom they lead?

A number of years ago, I started writing a series of short essays I called "trUTips." Leaders I worked with as a leadership and human resources consultant were constantly asking me for action plans. How could they turn leadership principles into measurably improved performance by their teams? What practical steps could they take that would move their teams from talking about excellence to producing excellent results for everyone in the value chain, both upstream and downstream from their team? I didn't want to give them grand schemes that would be difficult to implement, so the trUTips consisted of focused, discrete, actionable steps that could bring about immediate incremental improvement. Over several years, I published dozens of trUTips and got positive feedback from leaders who were getting good results within their teams. Eventually, I bundled the trUTips I had written up to that point and published them as an ebook (***www.thetrugroup.com/tru-tips/***). It's a great resource for any leader looking for ideas they can easily and quickly implement.

But the questions that led to the trUTips only led to more, bigger questions. Why is it so hard for some leaders to follow through on easy-to-understand principles like those behind the trUTips? While these principles are building collaboration, what might be simultaneously eroding it? Aside from these focused action steps, what sort of cultivatable habits create a climate for collaboration and performance?. Those questions led to this book. In it, we'll tackle these questions one at a time. After beginning by sharing my premises and presumptions, we'll look at something I call "Ought-But-Not Leadership." Ought-But-Not Leaders know the right thing to do in managing their teams—they just don't follow through consistently. Why not? I'll share some insights into this paradox that I've gleaned from my work with leaders and teams. Next, we'll look at some of the most dangerous threats to a successfully collaborating team. Finally, we'll examine four habits that leaders and teams should cultivate in order to keep from backsliding into the same old behaviors.

If you are a leader, there are constants that come with the role. Day in and day out you will be faced with big decisions that could have a huge impact on your team, and perhaps the larger organization around you. When you do make a decision, the feedback often gets personal, with people objecting to or arguing about the decision. You will, occasionally, face personal attacks from people outside of the decision-making loop. Collaboration is a garden that grows slowly, but misunderstanding and distrust are weeds that spring up overnight.

I don't believe in cure-all medicines or one-size-fits-all solutions. Every leader and every team is unique, so this book isn't intended as a simple prescription for success. But while there may be no magic pill that can make a draft horse win the Kentucky Derby, we can identify common traits that all thoroughbreds have. And while not all successful leaders and teams do everything the same way, they do have many things in common. What I've tried to do here is identify some of those common elements that contribute to their success, as well as some of the common traits that trip up teams that fail to reach their potential.

What are those elements common to successful leaders and teams? If I had to boil it down, I'd say that successful leaders build relationships with their people and have conversations that will lead to the performance their organization needs. If that sounds simple, it is. If it sounds simplistic, I'd argue that while successful collaboration has many components, failed collaboration is usually caused by a short list of factors. Chief among those are leaders who don't build constructive and collaborative relationships. In other words, the team doesn't collaborate because the leader doesn't collaborate or create a culture of collaboration. Why? Usually, because the leader and team can't honestly and constructively communicate. To put it another way, while collaborative relationships and constructive communication don't guarantee success, their absence strongly correlates with failure.

Honest conversations lead to thoughtful actions
and improved performance.

99

In fact, if I did try to articulate anything like a formula for leaders and team to succeed, it would be this: honest conversations lead to thoughtful actions and improved performance.Simple? Sure. But how often have you worked in a place where honest conversations that eventually led to improved performance actually occurred on a regular basis? I'm guessing that you've worked in plenty of teams and organizations where nothing of the sort ever occurred. Why not? If this formula is so simple and so obvious, why doesn't it happen more often in the real world?

The premise of this formula is that success for the leader happens as a result of the commitment and skills of their people. If the leader wants to get the best out of his or her people, for the team to become more than just the sum of its parts, it will require constructive conversations and collaborative relationships. A relationship, by definition, is not good or bad, it is just how we are connected. So just going about building relationships is a neutral activity. What defines a relationship is the adjective that people assign to this activity. What complicates this is the fact that, by definition, a relationship requires two or more people, all of whom are asked to assign their own adjective to this shared thing they have created called a relationship. They cannot assign common value to the relationship without honest conversation, the exchanging of thoughts in a way that builds up the team instead of dividing it with conflict. It's a complicated process, but that's what this book is about. I hope you find it helpful.

Chapter 1

I Believe...

Your beliefs become your thoughts,
Your thoughts become your words,
Your words become your actions,
Your actions become your habits,
Your habits become your values,
Your values become your destiny.
Gandhi

Genuine objectivity, at least when discussing anything to do with leading or organizing people, is a myth. Everyone brings a perspective to the subject. That perspective is shaped by our place in the world and how we got to it. It is embedded with preferences and prejudices, whether we recognize them or not (and, if we do not recognize them in ourselves, others might). We can't have a truly unbiased conversation about how leaders should lead and how teams should collaborate. We're always working from a set of beliefs and premises that influence our opinions and advice.

So, it only seems fair, before I dispense advice on the subject, for me to be honest and let you know where I am coming from. Neither one of us wants me to share my life story, but let me at least share my foundational beliefs about leadership and teamwork. Everything I write in this book rests on these beliefs, and if you don't accept my premises, you may be puzzled by my conclusions.

Why do I believe these things? They arise out of my life and career experiences, the inclinations of my basic personality type, and my sense of what's right and wrong.

Not everyone shares all of my premises. That's their right, but it is only honest for me to start by flying my flag, so to speak, and declaring my allegiance to these concepts. I encourage anyone who disagrees with them to articulate their own premises so we can have a constructive conversation about what is best for leaders and teams in the twenty-first-century value-oriented marketplace.

So, without further ado, here is what I believe about how people can and should work together.

1. Great Conversations Start with a Question

Something magical happens when we ask people a question: they start talking. Actually, when two people start asking and answering questions, the magic of conversation works a magic inside of us. In a recent research study (Wall Street Journal), scientists watched the activity in the human brain during different situations. They noticed that the act of talking about ourselves produces the same neurological effect as eating a meal or receiving money. That means that telling our story—opening up to be known by another person— is a basic human need and powerful stimulant. So, why don't we do it more often? There are lots of reasons, but one is surely that we rarely get permission to tell our story, because no one genuinely asks us who and how we are.

Open-ended questions create space for people to share what they are thinking, what is important to them right now, or their opinions on a topic. These questions always start with What? or How? The magic behind a great open-ended question is that it pulls out important information that leads to a rich and significant dialogue. I call this an "honest conversation."

Here are some examples of honest conversation starters:

- *"What are your top three priorities this week?"*
- *"How is the business running?"*
- *"What were some highlights from your weekend?"*

Conversely, questions that begin with Why? or poorly worded questions (for example, questions that use the word "you" in them) infer perceptions on our part and pull people out of problem-solving mode and into self-preservation mode. For example, questions like:

- *"Why did your team miss the production goal?"*
- *"How could you let this happen?"*
- *"Are you an idiot?"*

When we start a conversation by asking a great question, we bring others into the discussion from the beginning and make a habit out of the old axiom: Seek first to understand before seeking to be understood.

Seek first to understand before seeking to be understood.

99

One of my favorite questions to jump start an honest conversation is, "What needs to get done?" This question spurs thought and get things moving without putting anyone on the defensive. However you do it, though, make it your goal to get people sharing about themselves and their perspective without making them feel interrogated or put up their shields.

2. Honest Conversations Are the Foundation of Great Relationships

I remember a conversation I had with a leader who spent ten minutes speculating about why someone on their team had done something the previous week that caused lots of extra work for the leader and derailed some key work from getting completed. When I asked him what reasons the individual had given for their actions, they replied, "I'm not sure. I haven't asked them yet." This was an extremely busy leader, and he spent hours trying to guess why a member had derailed the rest of the team's work that week. The question and answer would have taken minutes, but the wondering and worry had wasted hours. It made no practical sense, but it is far too typical of how far some otherwise bright people will go to avoid having an honest conversation.

There are very few secrets in great relationships. What secrets (I'd prefer the word "confidences") that exist are offset by the equity of trust that is present, and they allow work to continue because people are given the benefit of the doubt. Another way to look at honesty is using the word transparency. Our actions are transparent when people know the Why? behind them. Change management is a critical skill for leaders, and one of the key pillars of managing change is focusing on making sure the Why? is crystal clear throughout the effort.

A leader once challenged my focus on transparency. He said that, when it came to firing someone, "You cannot tell people the truth in that situation." I concurred—the termination meeting isn't the time for building transparency and trust. Actually, it's usually the lack of those elements that brought you to that point in the first place. But I pushed back against the leader who made that comment. I told him I am less concerned with the transparency in that one situation, and more concerned with the transparency in one hundred decisions that happened before that conversation. If there had been more transparency early on, there would be less need to obscure, cover up, and defend when things became too badly broken to go on.

I told him I am less concerned with the transparency in that one situation, and more concerned with the transparency in one hundred decisions that happened before that conversation.

Trust is like a savings account. Every time we do something positive, communicate the Why? to someone in a constructive way, get input where needed, and follow through on what we said we would do, we make a deposit. As leaders, there will be times when we cannot share the whole story, and those are the moments when we make a withdrawal from that trust bucket. Withdrawals are only possible if there is a positive balance. Trust does not have overdraft protection. Honest conversations make trust possible, and they are the foundation of great relationships.

It is also important that the phrase "being liked" is not part of this premise. Peter Drucker once framed relationships a different way by saying, "The existence of trust does not necessarily mean they like one another, it means they understand one another." Honesty, not being liked, is the foundation of great conversations and effective relationships.

> *The existence of trust does not necessarily mean they like*
> *one another, it means they understand one another.*
>
> Peter Drucker

99

3. Leadership Is Working with People

Far too often, we look to action heroes or iconic historical figures for leadership models. When names like Abraham Lincoln, Martin Luther King, Jr., Ghandi, or Steve Jobs are mentioned, it makes leadership seem like an epic club that only titans can join.

When we use iconic historical figures as our leadership models, we are following an abstraction. We've never met these people, and our image of them is built on secondhand information. We have no context for the anecdotes we hear about them. It's hard to connect the legends about them with our ordinary work.

So, if you manage an accounts payable group, a steel construction crew, a technology implementation team, or even a twenty-five person business, do you think of yourself as a leader like the heroes described in leadership books and speeches? Maybe, but who do you look up to as the leader you want to be like? A key point in the development of any leader is to get them to shift their focus from the work of dealing with all the work in front of them and pause to look around. A great conversation for a new leader starts with these questions:

- *"What name comes to mind when you think of leadership?"*
- *"What are the things they did that makes you consider them a great leader?"*
- *"How are you like them? What can you do to be more like them?"*

When I started my own journey to develop as a leader, I was fortunate to have a few leaders who showed a commitment to what was best for me. Of course, I also had to learn to work with a few who viewed me as nothing more than a game piece to be used where needed. Through those experiences and what I learned from them, I have settled on a definition of leadership provided by Ken Blanchard: "Leadership is working with people to accomplish their goals and the goals of the organization."

> *Leadership is working with people to accomplish their goals and the goals of the organization.*
>
> Ken Blanchard

99

Whenever I share this one I ask the group, "What words stand out for you in this definition?" Invariably, they go right to "with people," "their goals," and "goals of organization." It is not a new concept to think of leadership as something we have to get others involved in, not just telling them what to do. Yet, when things start moving quickly in our work, and the changing landscape in which we operate seems to shift on a daily basis, the leadership I see most often is oriented toward directing and controlling. This style becomes a problem when things get too big for a single person to control.

So what is your definition of leadership?

Leaders have to make a choice about how they want to lead, and use feedback from others as their guide to making that their style. When we don't make a choice we will react to what happens, and our habits will be driven by getting things done now. We will get lost in our work of doing, and becoming the leader we want to be will not happen.

A leader once summed it up for me: "So, what you're telling me is that intentions without actions equals squat!" Great intentions are not leadership, at least not to those who matter: your people.

4. Fear Motivates Only for the Short Term, But Love Motivates for the Long Term

I shared this with a leadership group, and one of the leaders raised his hand and said, "So you're telling me that I have to love my people more? I just went through harassment training and heard that love gets leaders in trouble!" Of course, the group laughed, and I did smile. My response was twofold: "First, I am not a life coach, and I do not do any marital or family counseling. But second, let me ask you a question to start an honest conversation: What is love?"

It's not an academic or romantic question, but a very practical one. Does "loving your coworkers" mean inappropriate sexual comments or behavior? Of course not. But it might be about lightening someone's workload as they care for their terminally ill spouse, or facilitating a baby or wedding shower over lunch.

The ancient Greeks had at least two words for love: eros and agape. Eros was sexual passion. In human resources, harassment is rarely or never about sex itself; it's about the situation that the sexual behavior creates. Inappropriate sexual behaviors in the workplace create situations that are risky for the business and negative for the people that work there. When I say love, I'm not talking about sexual eros, but agape, which is selfless love. Agape is love that puts the needs of others above our own. It is the love we see in families and friendships. When we care for people, we create the possibility that they will also care for us and others at a level much deeper than the daily to-do list we call our work. When we focus only on the work and drive accountability by always asking, "Why did this not get done?" we put the work before the person.

Do you believe that people work harder when they feel like someone loves them? I work with people who believe that, and I help them develop the habits and abilities to make it a reality in their lives and workplaces.

5. Everyone Has the Potential to Be Amazing at a Job

Everyone has the potential to be amazing at a job. It might not be the job they are actually occupying today, but there is some job where they can contribute, maybe even shine.

I shared this with a group and hands instantly shot up.

- *"So, what you are saying, Scott, is that everyone can work and be productive. I think the welfare numbers and homeless numbers contradict that statement."*
- *"What about the pharmacist with the drug problem who used to be great at his job?"*
- *"What about the special needs adult? They can't be a policeman."*

The ensuing conversation consisted of the group trying to shoot down my idea, imagining all the reasons people can't do work. In the end, the conversation actually proved my point. I believe that it is important to focus on what people can do instead of constantly talking about what they cannot do. This is not easy, as proven by the Americans with Disabilities Act and how long it has taken us to implement something that is based on the belief that all people have value and should have access to things (work, recreation, bathrooms) regardless of who they are.

The second part of this belief is that it makes me inquisitive about what everyone is capable of, both in terms of what they have done and what they have not tried yet. This leads to my definition of performance: Performance = Talent + Passion + Work.

$$Performance = Talent + Passion + Work$$

99

We all possess talents that make certain things easy for us, and when we understand what those are and build on them, we are capable of amazing things. Do we have limitations and weaknesses? Absolutely, and in some cases they bar us from certain kinds of work. Think of the supermarket greeter—can you show up for work, smile, and focus on helping everyone walking through the door feel welcome? Some people would be incapable of doing that job because they don't have the Gallup-defined talent of "WOO" (Winning Others Over).

Passion also acts like a fuel for our work, and when we are cultivating those passions, they create energy for us. This does not mean only at work, because for many work has to get out of the way of the things we are passionate about: family, service work, hobbies, friendships. Whatever they are, if our passions are being fulfilled they become a great source of energy for other parts of our work.

In the end, talents and passions are just potential until we do the work of building the skills and experience around them to make performance happen. Our path to mastery is built on hard work. In his book Outliers, Malcolm Gladwell shares research pointing to the fact that it takes 10,000 hours of work to master your craft. For true performance, talent is the foundation, passion is the fuel, and the work is what makes it happen.

6. Individuals Own Development, Organizations Own Support

There are some great leadership lessons that can be learned through parenting. One happens to people between the age of thirteen and their early twenties. Learning shifts to something owned by the child because it becomes their work and is now too big for their parents. If you are a parent and have tried to help your children with advanced math or grammar, you have probably experienced this. When kids become smarter than we are in a subject, helping them is often not an option. The second leadership lesson parenting teaches us is that kids will inevitably grow away from us more and more, making it impossible to make decisions for them. Leaders need to raise their team so that, over time, team members can make and own the consequences of their decisions.

Think of parenting older children up against the definition of leadership I offered: Leadership is working with people (the child) to accomplish their goals (might be fuzzy—an A, passing the class, getting you off their back, hanging out with their friends, saving enough to buy a car, etc.) and the goals of the organization (moving out and starting to live their own life, still needing my love but not my money).

Business is like parenting, and the goal is to produce some sort of result, whether it is profit, a product, or delivery of a service. A big key to making leadership easier is recognizing the boost you get as a leader when the individuals in your business start to own the work. Much of my work is with growing organizations where founders need to create a leadership team around them to provide leadership because the business has gotten too big for them to manage on their own.

Individual development mirrors leading a business, because it takes sustained effort over time and will not get done without individual ownership. I believe that for it to happen the individual has to own the development plan and the organization has to own the support.

By providing support, leaders also send a clear message that you matter (that's why love matters in the workplace), which becomes a way to keep your talented people in your organization. People stay places where they are getting an opportunity to do what they do best and feel supported. The responsibility of the individual is to do the work and to get better, because the organization will only be successful if they become more efficient and effective at their work. The organization soars when people not only own their work, but look to solve little problems before they become big problems.

7. In Great Organizations, Everyone Leads
One of the biggest frustrations entrepreneurs experience in growing organizations is the constant current of problems they have to swim against. When I ask them who their best people are, they point towards the people that grab the work and go. When I ask what "go" means, they say something like this:

"My best people have a way of quickly knowing what outcome is desired and figuring out a way to get there without a lot of help. My conversations with them tend to center around them struggling with a couple of different solutions they have developed for bigger problems because they have solved all the little problems."

In the end, leaders get work done. They see the challenges and problems in the work, and they figure out a way to move past/through them to achieve a goal. That is personal leadership, whether it is in customer service, at the reception desk, from the chief financial officer, or from the president. Successful companies are full of leaders. Companies that want to grow and continue to be successful have to figure out a way to build a culture where everyone is expected to lead and are given the support to become leaders in what they do.

A great example of this was Google in its early years. That company developed a longstanding tradition of giving people a set amount of time to work on anything they wanted. Great ideas emerged because people made choices to focus efforts on something they saw as a problem/opportunity and made it happen. Google translated their need for a culture of innovation and leadership into the habit of time to lead. In great organizations, the culture promotes ownership and leadership, and those are the people that stay around.

8. Trust Is a Gift

As a consultant, and before that an HR professional, I often experience a strange phenomenon when I go into a new area or project. I call it the "whispers," and as soon as people hear I am coming in from the outside to help build culture or develop leaders, it begins.

- *"What you really need to know, Scott, is that their leadership style is the problem."*
- *"I don't want to gossip, but you do know the two of them had a relationship a couple of years ago that has been very disruptive."*
- *"The big issue is that they are the owner, and yet for the last two years they are only here one or two days a week, and when they do show-up they undo many of our decisions. As a result, we just stopped making them."*

I respond by saying, "It sounds like that is a pretty significant issue for you. How comfortable are you sharing it with them?"

Almost always, the answer is, "I'm not comfortable at all. I don't want to get fired."

Trust is a gift. When things bother us or we have a conflict between our life's priorities, it is something that has to be talked about (i.e. honest conversation). It's not easy. It takes courage. Being able to do it is about trusting the person you are delivering it to. Trust is the thing that takes hours to build and seconds to destroy.

Leaders, when someone shares something with you that exposes something that is extremely personal or is an observation of something you are doing that could make you mad enough to fire them, you are being given the gift of trust. Trust is a big topic, and one practice I give to leaders that want to better gauge the level of trust in their group is to spend a week listening for people disagreeing with them, giving them direct feedback on their leadership behaviors, or sharing sensitive personal information.

At the end of the week, this will give you an indication of how much trust is present. If you have accumulated a measurable amount of these gifts, that is a positive sign. What you do with them is a great foundation for developing as a manager and a leader. That is the work of the leader. If there are no gifts collected, that is another great place to start, but the work is probably going to be harder.

This thought is the foundation of my performance mantra: honest conversations lead to thoughtful actions and improved performance.

99

My message to all individuals on the team: If you choose not to share sensitive information or opinions, that is your choice, but you are leaving it up to your leader to make decisions with the best available information. If you keep information to yourself, you also need to be accepting of any decisions that are made.

Trust is a gift, and when those gifts are being given freely, being opened and followed-up on, positive cultures are being built. This thought is the foundation of my performance mantra: honest conversations lead to thoughtful actions and improved performance.

9. A, B, and C Players Exist in All Organizations

As the 2008/2009 recession began to subside, a leader shared with me this view of his organization: "Scott, the one positive thing that came out of the last downturn was that we were able to shed part of our B-players and all of our C-players. The team we have left is mostly A-players." He was so sure that he was right, but he was so very, very wrong.

Life happens, and performance is impacted. Organizational change happens, and every time we go through a change that moves people out of an organization or moves resources that people need to do their jobs, their attitude is impacted. Think of these cause and effect statements:

Action: Positions are eliminated
Effect: Work is absorbed by the remaining team members

Action: Processes are made more efficient
Effect: Jobs disappear or individuals in those roles have to learn new skills

To clarify, I am saying that when you remove your C-players from your organization, they will be replaced by others. As an example, remember the talent management practice made famous by Jack Welch at GE of force ranking people each year and removing the bottom 10%? Did anyone ever ask where those 10% came from? This type of churn creates a situation that turns A-players into B-players and B-players into C-players. To believe anything else is not an honest conversation, it is dreaming.

This is another consequence of the impact of letting some of your top people go. At the height of the recession in 2009, HR Solutions did a survey about employee engagement. They found that 14% of actively engaged employees (your best people, the ones you consider high potentials/high performers) were worried about job loss. That number was 6% four years earlier. They also found that only 21% of actively disengaged employees (non-performers, those who do just enough or cleverly hide in the pack) were worried about their job, vs. 41% four years earlier.

This is a major reason that effective leadership development programs always address the topic of change management and communication with leaders. Remember, it takes a lot of leadership energy to fire people or force them to move to new roles in an organization. Too often, organizations of any size do not do it well, and the result is fear or uncertainty for people.

Hope > Fear + Anger + Frustration + Worry + Hunger + Weariness +

_____ + _____

99

I use the following equation with people in transition, urging them to manage themselves to ensure that: *Hope > Fear + Anger + Frustration + Worry + Hunger + Weariness +* _____ + _____.

Performance based on hope allows us to move forward. A-players have an attitude and commitment that allows them to process fear and uncertainty in a healthy way and move forward, which is why they stand out. However, when we repeatedly ask individuals to find the resources to rebalance this equation, some don't. It might only be 8%, as illustrated in our example above, but that is still one out of ten people. That becomes the fuel for Jack Welch's 10% yearly churn.

There you have it: the nine premises that will form the foundation my discussion of leadership in this book. Now that we have the foundation laid, let's move on to answering an important and puzzling question: "If we all have some idea of what actions will make us great leaders, why aren't there more terrific leaders in this world?"

Big Ideas from Chapter 1

- *Leadership begins with core beliefs about people and how they can and should work together.*
- *Writing and sharing your core beliefs is a foundation to others understanding you.*
- *In summary, here are my nine core beliefs about leadership, people, and relationships:*
  1. *Great conversations start with a question*
  2. *Honest conversations is the formation of great relationships*
  3. *Leadership is working with people*
  4. *Fear motivates only for the short term, but love motivates for the long term*
  5. *Everyone has the potential to be amazing at a job*
  6. *Individuals own development, organizations own support*
  7. *In great organizations, everyone leads*
  8. *Trust is a gift*
  9. *A, B. and C players exist in all organizations*

Make Your Action Plan

What is your definition of leadership? (one sentence)

What are your core beliefs about people?

-
-
-

What are your core beliefs about relationships at work or healthy teams?

-
-
-

What other core beliefs are foundational for you as a leader/team member?

Chapter 2
Ought But Nots

Trust is equal parts character and competence . . .
You can look at any leadership failure, and it's always a
failure of one or the other.
Stephen M. R. Covey

We are what we repeatedly do.
Aristotle

When I sat down to begin writing this book, I decided that I wouldn't just give a list of tried, true, and tired advice. You know what I mean: plan more, procrastinate less, be proactive, put first things first, etc., etc., etc.

If you're reading this, you probably have a job that requires you to lead others. You're also clearly an intellectually curious leader who looks for resources to help you be more effective in your career. Given that profile, this is almost certainly not the first book you've ever read on performance and professional development. I'll bet that you've read plenty of articles and listened to plenty of lectures, covered some of these topics in school or professional training, and most likely have attended a conference or two where gifted speakers gave you all sorts of advice about how to become better at what you do. Any serious business professional today has received no shortage of advice about how to compete and improve.

Given all that, I have a simple question: If we all know so much about what we ought to do to compete and improve, why do we not actually follow through on all these great ideas? In my career in human resources and entrepreneurial consulting, I have seen bright people who know better fail to practice what they preach and perform according to their principles. They rarely needed to be told what they ought to do; they needed to understand why they were not implementing the obvious. They also needed help overcoming whatever resistance that was coming from inside or outside of them that kept them from carrying out what they knew they should be doing. It's not unlike physical fitness: most bright people would say that most of us would be healthier if we ate less and healthier foods, while exercising and sleeping more. We know what we ought to do; it's not a complicated formula. But if it's so simple, why don't more of us do it?

Ought-But-Not Leaders are often simply ignorant of how their own actual behavior differs from the principles they espouse.

99

Over time, I developed a term for this type of manager (which is all of us sometimes): an Ought-But-Not Leader. An Ought-But-Not Leader feels frustrated that he or she isn't performing to expectations, but can't exactly articulate why. An Ought-But-Not Leader has a shelf full of books on leadership, a well-organized planner, and works plenty of hours. But the performance principles they intellectually ascribe to aren't producing the results they or others expect. Why? Do they need another book? Well, maybe this one, because in this chapter I'm going to identify some of the most common reasons for the gap between what Ought-But-Not Leaders know and what they actually do. I will answer the question, "What makes potentially great leaders into Ought-But-Not Leaders?"

1. Ought-But-Not Leaders Think They Are Great, Even When They Aren't

The first explanation for the paradox of Ought-But-Not Leaders is simply a lack of self-awareness. Many of them think they are planning, prioritizing, and being proactive. They are absolutely convinced they are building positive relationships with their team, communicating effectively, and giving useful feedback. They are genuinely confused by the lack of results. They aren't hypocrites, because hypocrisy implies an intentional refusal to live up to the standards one sets for others. No, Ought-But-Not Leaders are often simply ignorant of how their own actual behavior differs from the principles they espouse.

In his book The Speed of Trust, Stephen M.R. Covey observes that, "We judge ourselves by our intentions and others by their behavior." In other words, Ought-But-Not Leaders feel justified because they mean well and try hard. They might not accept that explanation from a coworker, direct report, or vendor, but they have a genuine blind spot when it comes to their own actions.

> *We judge ourselves by our intentions and*
> *others by their behavior.*
>
> Stephen M. R. Covey

99

I did a 360-survey once with a very successful leader. She looked at her role and rated what she did well and where she could improve. She also received that same feedback from her leader, peers, and team. The strong message from all those around her was that she was good at what she did, but she didn't listen to the opinions of others and didn't care about the people she worked with. When I reviewed the survey results with her, I watched the Kübler-Ross five stages of grief and loss play out across her face: denial, anger, bargaining, depression, and finally acceptance. Her actions did not align with her beliefs. The feedback also revealed something even more critical: she was ignorant of how the people around her saw and interpreted her performance.

The Merriam-Webster dictionary defines ignorance as "a lack of knowledge, education, or awareness." In contrast, it defines stupid as "having or showing a lack of ability to learn and understand things." The fine line between being ignorant and stupid is the ability to learn. What is often revealed in a 360 is that self-deception exists because leaders think they are doing the things that align with how they feel, but their people are not seeing it.

The definition of ignorance is "a lack of knowledge, education, or awareness." In contrast the definition of stupid is defined as "having or showing a lack of ability to learn and understand things."

99

In the previous chapter, I said that I believe that great conversations start with a question. Another way to say this is that great conversations give both leaders and followers a chance to test for ignorance, and an opportunity to avoid being thought of as stupid. I know stupid is a harsh word in our politically correct world, but when we think we are doing the obvious right thing, but aren't, we need a conversation that wakes us up. Self-deception is dangerous for anyone, but it is fatal for a leader.

Think of how the 360 example above gave that leader a chance to test for ignorance and remove it from her relationships. The core questions both leaders and the people around them are answering are basically:

- *What am I doing well?*
- *What is one thing I could improve on to be more effective at my job?*

Hearing this kind of feedback is never easy, at least for most of us. One reason is that we want those around us to credit us for our intentions. Our intentions are real to us, and they matter as expressions of our values and beliefs. Doesn't everyone see that we care about these things? But the agape love we spoke about in the last chapter is more than a feeling. It is love in action, putting the needs of others above your own. Expressed in the workplace, it asks whether the leader develops people because she wants them to succeed or because she wants to use them to succeed herself. When it is the latter, there is dissonance between principles and practice, but the Ought-But-Not Leader herself can rarely see it. She is blindsided by feedback because she honestly believes she is doing the right thing, all because she means to do the right thing.

A big part of the follow-up to a 360 is having someone to help a leader effectively make the changes they need to make based on the feedback they receive. When I step into that role as an executive coach, my goal is to ensure that the actions taken demonstrate that the leader has the ability to learn and change, and demonstrates that to their team. Obviously, Ought-But-Not Leaders are never asked to stand up in front of their teams and say, "I may be ignorant, but I am not stupid." But being able to say, "I am sorry, I thought that we were aligning our values and practice more closely," and then following that with an adjusted plan of action, replaces ignorance with a demonstrated ability to learn—which proves that the Ought-But-Not Leader isn't stupid.

Let me address one more thing: the frustration of the Ought-But-Not Leader who has a lot on their plate and interprets the constant pressure to always be adjusting to the needs of their teams as a battle they cannot win. I once had an Ought-But-Not Leader push back, and the conversation sounded like this:

Leader: So Scott, what you are telling me is that I always have to be thinking about what my people are thinking when I'm making decisions? I make hundreds of those a day as a leader, and I can't do my job if I'm always worrying about what they think.

Me: What makes this worrying?

Leader: You said to ask them questions and get their input? That sounds to me like worrying.

Me: Let me repeat what I am hearing. If I ask questions to the people that work for me before I make decisions, that will show them I am worried about what they think.

Leader: Yes.

Me: Let's turn this around and look at it from their perspective. If someone asks you your opinion on something and then uses your advice, how does it make you feel?

Leader: Good, because they valued my opinion and in the end I was right.

Me: What word would best describe how you think they feel about you?

Leader: They care what I think. [pause and eventual smile] Okay, I get it.

Me: It can't happen for every decision, I understand. But using it more will make a difference.

Ought-But-Not Leaders think they are when they aren't, and all of us are Ought-But-Not Leaders at some point. The ironic thing about getting feedback in this area is that there are things we are doing right, and leaders need to get that feedback, too.

The path out of ignorance requires learning and change, which takes energy. We get that energy by first celebrating what we do well, then translating that new awareness into habits that will help us be more effective leaders.

99

Your goal as a leader is to write a new chapter for yourself called I think I am, my team confirms that I am, and where I'm not, I will.

2. Ought-But-Not Leaders Have Fallen for the Illusion of Control

As a young leader, I remember receiving my first Franklin planner and taking the class to learn how to use it. I was hooked. I carried it everywhere, and eventually I got a fancy leather cover with a zipper so I could fit more stuff in there and be more organized. When the Palm Pilot technology was launched, I jumped on board and went electronic. Then I had four kids, joined an entrepreneurial organization, became an executive, and my planner (along with my head) exploded. I had NO TIME!

The funny thing is, I still have four kids, my own business, an amazing wife, two board memberships, and I still have no time. A time management class will not fix what ails me. I follow bloggers like Seth Godin and Ken Blanchard who give me tips on personal effectiveness, and time shows up routinely as a topic, but that won't fix my problem either.

In Ought-But-Not Leadership, not having time is an excuse, a dodge for deeper issues. It's easy to hide behind because who is going to argue with someone saying, "Sorry, I have to go to my son's soccer game" or, "I promised my wife that I would be home to celebrate our anniversary"? I teach time management using the classic "Who's Got The Monkey" article (Harvard Business Review), and I see and hear very real reasons why leaders can't do succession planning or performance evaluations. I get it. But becoming more effective at managing your time will not fix the problem of demands exceeding capacity. To be a professional in the modern world is a perpetual story of trying to fit more than twenty-four hours worth of priorities and responsibilities into our day.

Ought-But-Not Leaders are no busier than anyone else, but they don't recognize what's going on. They have fallen for an illusion of control. They believe they can plan, prioritize, and perform without having to take other people into account or make dynamic adjustments. When those around them point out that Ought-But-Not Leaders aren't following through, they need an external explanation—an excuse. Something other than them has to be to blame. The most convenient scapegoat is that they are exceptionally busy, or that unrealistic outside demands have intruded on their priorities.

Based on a study by Career Cast, here are the ten most stressful jobs and what they make:

1	Enlisted military personnel	$28,840
2	Military general	$196,300
3	Firefighter	$45,225
4	Airline pilot	$114,200
5	Event coordinator	$45,250
6	Public relations executive	$54,170
7	Corporate executive (senior)	$168,140
8	Newspaper reporter	$35,870
9	Police officer	$55,270
10	Taxi driver	$22,820

If you look at these jobs, there are two key themes. First, it is stressful to go to work at a job where your life is on the line. Secondly, it is stressful to do a job where you don't control what comes next because the nature of your job is often driven by outside influences (i.e. customers, events, etc.). Lots of jobs come with plenty of accountability, but not the control to completely manage outcomes. Think of the nonmilitary/public service jobs on this list: airline pilot, event coordinator, public relations executive, senior corporate executive, newspaper reporter, and taxi driver. Deadlines, crises, and customers make people in these roles feel like their time is not their own, which is stressful. Yet, can any of these jobs say that 100% of their time is out of their control? Is it safe to say that all these jobs control 50% of their time? What would be the impact of feeling like you controlled 70%?

Time is a big barrier to breaking out of being an Ought-But-Not Leader, yet it can be addressed by stepping back and reassessing one's priorities and real control of their time. One of the books I like to give leaders struggling with priorities is Tuesdays With Morrie by Mitch Albom, not so they will think about their own death, but to get someone else's answer to the question, "What's important?" and how that question changes when we have one final chance to set our priorities straight.

Another way to have the conversation that Morrie has without dying is to do the leadership development exercise of writing your own obituary. Here are the follow-up questions:

- *What are my priorities based on my obituary?*
- *What would my priorities be if you looked at my schedule today?*
- *Where am I in alignment?*
- *Where are my gaps?*

It is not realistic for most of us to control 100% of our time, but what would be the impact for controlling 10% more of our time so we can get to our stated priorities? We control more of our time than we think, yet it is sometimes stressful to control so little in our work. This list confirms it, and Ought-But-Not Leaders name time as a barrier and leave it there. That must change if they are to become more effective leaders.

3. Ought-But-Not Leaders Procrastinate and Do the Fun Stuff While Avoiding the Hard Stuff

Ought-But-Not Leaders have great plans, but they struggle to perform up to their promises because they procrastinate.

Why do we procrastinate?

I have a habit of developing weekly, monthly, and quarterly goals. I once set a goal for myself concerning cold calling, and on it was a name of someone I kind of knew. I had coached his daughter in soccer, and he was the CEO of a growing business. I delayed calling him for two months because I worried about what he would say, what I would say, and what my ask would be. Finally, I called him. He was warm, invited me to stop by, and ended up referring me to a couple of other potential business contacts. It was a fun conversation, and he provided me with some encouragement that I needed at that point in my life. I had spent two months worrying and procrastinating, and in the end it was a fun and enjoyable experience.

> *Resistance is a repelling force. It's negative. Its aim is to shove us away, distract us, prevent us from doing our work.*
>
> Stephen Pressfield

In Stephen Pressfield's book **Do The Work!,** he calls this "the Resistance." He says that, "Resistance is a repelling force. It's negative. Its aim is to shove us away, distract us, prevent us from doing our work." Understanding our procrastination means understanding the resistance that keeps us from doing things. As an executive coach, friend, father, and entrepreneur, procrastination shows up in many forms in my life, and it's probably the number-one contributing factor whenever I fail. The voice of procrastination varies, and it is actually embedded in my Ought-But-Not Leadership model:

- *"I talked to them about their performance evaluation."*
  (But really I didn't—it was in passing in the hallway for thirty seconds, and no follow-up happened.)
- *"I don't have time for cold calling, there are too many things my current clients need." (You mean the clients who are set after this year and will not be ordering more for six to twelve months?*
  By the way, you know your pipeline of new orders is empty, right?)

One powerful manifestation of the Resistance that Pressfield describes is labeling some things "fun" and other things "work." It's only natural to want to do the fun stuff. Those of us who play golf as a hobby can capture this paradox in two words: "the range." I know a few great golfers, and when you talk to them about how they got better, they always say the same thing: good golfers go to the range three or four times for every round they play. Their ratio of practice to play is almost four to one. But most weekend golfers see hitting balls on the range as work. We want to play because that's fun. So we pull into the parking lot, pull on our shoes, meet our buddies, and head to the first tee. I've often wondered if, in an effort to counter this tendency, courses should fill their practice ranges with targets like in a video game: old windows, doors, trampolines, old cars, a mobile home, etc. I think I could stay interested longer and get better. The point is that when we unconsciously think of some activities as fun and others as work, we're going to be unconsciously drawn to the fun things to the exclusion of the work.

What is the "practice range" in your work? If you are in sales, it's probably cold calling or role-playing sales calls with your teammates to get feedback and refine your approach. As a facilitator, I actually think role-playing ranks below actual cold calling on the fun activities list. I watch the resistance show up on people's faces when I ask them to find a partner and practice their script. They hate that work. I also hear their ironic comments after a couple of rounds of practice and feedback, after they gained confidence and skill in the practice sessions.

Another area of practice in our work is feedback. How many of you have sought out a teammate before a big presentation and said these words: "Jill, would you do a favor for me during my presentation? One thing I am really working on is not reading the slides, and using my words to tell a quick story or relate the point to the client's needs. Would you mind giving me some feedback as to how well I do that, and maybe give me one thing I could work on for my next presentation?" Why haven't you heard that very often? Because most of us think of giving a presentation as fun and getting feedback as work.

Whether it's having a difficult conversation, role-playing a difficult conversation, or soliciting feedback on your work, we get so caught up in the trap of focusing on the negative outcomes that we don't do anything. We might not use the words "fun" or "easy," but how we use our time and the actual work we focus on contains all the evidence needed to convict us of willful procrastination. This is not necessarily a conviction of wrong vs. right, because for many Ought-But-Not Leaders even the fun things have some value. No one is saying that they're playing video games in their office. But their work does flow down the path of least resistance. They could be convicted of losing the battle to face the resistance and do what they know they ought to do first.

How do we cure this? How do we make the important stuff also the fun stuff? When I work with leaders going through a career change, the first step is always for them to "own it." People need to recognize that the adjectives attached to their work are their adjectives, and in order to move through them and get to the work, they have to change the adjectives. This process is called "reframing." When we reframe things in our own mind, it puts us in a position to move through the resistance we create.

4. Ought-But-Not Leaders Are Tunnel-Visioned by Stress

It was a crisis. Our asthmatic daughter came down the stairs at 11:30 p.m., seemingly unable to breathe. Panic set in, and within seconds we were in the car wearing our pajamas, ready to blast out of the garage on our way to the emergency room. I hesitated while my wife anxiously asked what I was waiting for. I realized that I couldn't start the engine. I was a father in a crisis, needing to act for my family, and I had forgotten the keys. I was also missing my shoes, wallet, and cell phone. While our daughter struggled to breathe, I ran back to get them. In the meantime, my wife asked my daughter a few questions, the panic subsided, and we (or she) began to manage the crisis differently.

It's hard to think when you're under stress, much less to listen. Under stress, it's hard to sit back and ask the right questions that get to the root cause of a problem that is plaguing your team, even if that question is simply, "How would you propose solving this?" For example, when business is keeping you and your teams at work ten-plus hours a day, how often do these questions get asked:

- *What wins have you had today?*
- *What work is bogging you down?*
- *What can I do to support you?*

We know that when we ask #3 it could mean more work for us!

Dr. Roger Birkman spent fifty-plus years researching the space between usual behavior and stress behavior, and he captured it in an assessment called the Birkman Method®. His research produced the tools that help identify not only our usual behaviors, but our underlying needs that, if not met, will result in stress behaviors that put our relationships in jeopardy. As complex beings, we often assume our usual behaviors—such as being socially outgoing or thoughtful—get magnified under stress, so that we become more outgoing or thoughtful. But that's just an assumption we make because it's easy. The Birkman Method provides a lens that allows us to more easily see our actual behaviors under stress. Surprisingly, they aren't just exaggerations of our normal pattern.

Dr. Birkman shares one example of how we interact in our one-on-one relationships. Seventy percent of us provide more direct feedback than what we in turn need or want to receive from others. In other words, we like to critique others more than we want to be critiqued. I have a friend who's a "tell-it-like-it-is" guy. He let others know what he thinks about their work, and he let the chips lie where they fall. I'm sure you know the type. Anyway, one time I saw him behaving in some ways that I felt were negatively impacting a project and his team, so I gave him some feedback. I thought I did it concisely and professionally, but his reaction surprised me. For all of the critiques he had dished out to others, he really couldn't take receiving any himself. His feelings were hurt, he got real quiet, and the conversation ended quickly.

We all need some sort of feedback, and the Birkman Method does a great job highlighting that our needs often differ from our normal behaviors. In the heat of battle it is often hard to understand that, especially when we add in the dynamic of team. I was using this method to help a leadership team understand their strengths and weaknesses as a team, and the output from the tool told them that when they were working under stress they became hyper-focused on tasks and much less focused on their people. As a result, their communication style probably became more of a tell style and less of a listening style. They all looked at each other and smiled uncomfortably. The leader then shared that they had just received feedback from an employee survey that the employees were not getting enough communication about how the business was doing and what the priorities were.

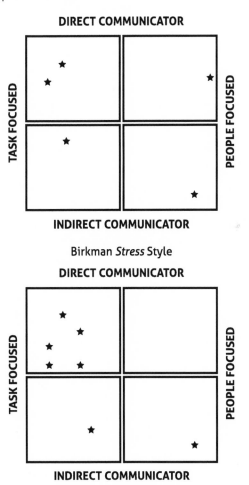

DIRECT COMMUNICATOR

TASK FOCUSED

PEOPLE FOCUSED

INDIRECT COMMUNICATOR

Birkman *Stress* Style

DIRECT COMMUNICATOR

TASK FOCUSED

PEOPLE FOCUSED

INDIRECT COMMUNICATOR

That might be true as an individual, but my follow-up question is, "How does your stress impact your ability to manage others?" Are thoughtful actions based on honest conversations or what you think is the right thing to do? The team I mentioned above kept doing, but stopped listening and sharing. Ought-But-Not Leadership is exposed during stressful times. It is during these times that we must focus on the simple things that will help us and others address their core needs and move back to a more usual and productive state of behavior in spite of the stressful conditions. This is the essence of something we will talk more about: self-management.

I think back to my example of a medical emergency. The question I have learned to ask myself (and have asked my wife to ask me) is, "Do you have your wallet, your keys, and your phone?" That single question slows me down for a few seconds during a rush out the door, and it has allowed me a chance to reset my current state and not forget some key things I need to be productive at that moment.

Another way to look at our intentional actions during stress is through the lens of being mindful and deliberate. Mindfulness is the fun part about getting to know yourself and those around you. It is when you know the strengths and the stress behaviors that will show up. I think of how my family manages me during the packing of the car, when I get hyper-focused on making everything fit and ask for no surprise additions. I think of the mindful and deliberate actions I take to set a target of thirty minutes before I feel like we have to leave, so last-second bathroom breaks or walks around the house allow us time to leave focused on the excitement of the coming journey and not the presence of a stressed-out father.

5. Ought-But-Not Leaders Are Afraid that if They Tell the Truth, Others Will Leave

"We have worked together for several months now, and I don't believe you have the ability to do what we need you to do in this role. I have to make a change."

How many of you have had to initiate a conversation like this? These are not easy words to say. Usually, the internal resistance that Pressfield describes becomes almost impossible to push through. Most of us really hate confronting a direct report of uncomfortable truth, and we will put up with a lot of frustration to avoid having to pull the trigger and make a change. Why is it so hard to be honest with someone who works for you or with you? In my years as a coach and consultant to leaders, I have walked with leaders through some very difficult situations that have taken weeks and sometimes months to resolve. They knew what they had to do, but they couldn't bring themselves to do it. It was almost the very definition of Ought-But-Not Leadership. I've become convinced that Ought-But-Not Leaders hear something like one of these statements in his or her head as they work up the courage to have a difficult conversation:

- *"I hired you, and to fire you so quickly means I made a mistake."*
- *"I believe that leadership is about supporting your people to ensure their success, and to fire you means I have failed. I do not fail, so I need to try harder."*
- *"They are family (cousin, brother, parent), and having this conversation will ruin our family Thanksgiving or Christmas celebrations."*
- *"They are a friend. Our families are intertwined and we live in a small town, so this conversation would upset more than just a work relationship."*
- *"Who would take a job with less money? I know their financial*

situation, and they would never agree to that."

- *"I have so much work, and if they leave my life will be more miserable. Let's wait until we are through this project, because they can at least help with that."*

In the end, the resistance is centered around the simple thought that, "If I am honest, they will leave." I will even add another extended thought to that: "If I am honest, they will not only leave, they will not like me, they will think I am a bad leader, and I will feel guilty because I failed them."

Ought-But-Not Leaders get hung up on the premise that, "When people fail, the leader has failed." In my experience, although the resistance centers itself around the big conversations, what is actually missing is many of the little honest conversations that help make this big conversation smaller. Think about that: we actually make this big event bigger because we don't have some of the smaller conversations that become little moments of caring:

- *Pausing meetings to say thank you and recognize great work*
- *Paying for little things (meat for a cookout) because the team needs a break*
- *Remembering names of kids/spouses*
- *Never missing a one-on-one, and with it giving them feedback on performance (both positive and negative)*
- *Going out of your way to celebrate things that matter to your people, from a demolition derby victory at the county fair to a child getting a college scholarship*
- *Sending birthday notes to people at home*

It should be hard to ask someone to step down from a role or leave the organization. Honesty is hard, and a commitment to agape love does not make it easier. However, a commitment to agape love makes it easier on the rest of the team, because all of the little moments of caring have added up and told a story where the perception of you as a leader who cares is cemented.

Disney ruined our expectations for the outcomes of an honest conversation: everyone does not always live happily ever after. Yet, when we make honesty our goal, and when things like agape love, truth, and trust become our visible motives, our actions tend to provide a narrative that gives others a different perspective to bring into some of these big conversations.

Conclusion

The Greek philosopher Socrates was famous for making the words carved over the oracle at Delphi his motto and mission: "Know Thyself." Ought-But-Not Leaders are puzzled by why their principles and plans don't produce the results they expect. They are always looking for an external explanation or convenient scapegoat. The truth is often even closer than in front of them—it's inside of them.

The process of aligning actions and ideals begins with honest self-discovery. In this chapter, I've outlined five of the major reasons why Ought-But-Not Leaders experience this gap between their principles and practices. Honestly examine yourself to see where your mindset is turning you into an Ought-But-Not Leader, and then commit to change. Don't spend another day giving in to the resistance and neglecting to improve your own performance and that of their team.

Big Ideas from Chapter 2

- *There is almost universal agreement that people will work harder when they are treated with respect, kindness, and commitment to their success. The real issue is that leaders fail to consistently demonstrate these beliefs in their actions.*
- *An Ought-but-Not Leader is a leader who knows what they need to do but struggles with the follow through.*
- *Successful leaders recognize the barriers disrupting their effectiveness as a leader, and they find a way to break through those barriers.*
- *Here are the key barriers that cause people to become Ought-But-Not Leaders:*
    1. *They think they are being effective leaders when they are not (in the eyes of their team).*
    2. *They have fallen for the illusion of control. It is not about being a better planner, it is about being better at prioritizing.*
    3. *They procrastinate by doing the fun stuff and not the hard stuff.*
    4. *They are tunnel-visioned by stress.*
    5. *They are afraid that if they tell the truth others would leave.*

Make Your Action Plan

Question to ask yourself	Your answer
1. I have received direct feedback in the last 12 months from my team that I am being an effective leader.	Yes/No
2. I review and reset my priorities at least weekly and meet with my full team each week to help them do the same.	Yes/No
3. There are not difficult conversations or decisions that I am procrastinating on right now.	Yes/No
4. Stress is not negatively impacting my leadership right now.	Yes/No
5. I am not holding back giving feedback to someone right now because I am worried they will leave if I am truthful	Yes/No

Any question that you answered "No" to needs to be addressed so it does not cause any more damage to your effectiveness as a leader. An advanced application of this is to pick someone you work with that you trust, and ask them to answer these for you as a way of gathering feedback.

In making your action plan, ask yourself, "What would it take for me to move from "No" to "Yes?" Pick one question and fix it. When that is done fix the next one. Repeat weekly or monthly.

Chapter 3
Threats

The emotional brain responds to an event more quickly than the thinking brain.

Daniel Golman

Most people do not listen with the intent to understand; they listen with the intent to reply.

Stephen Covey

So far, we've looked at the basic elements I believe contribute to a collaborative culture and better performance by teams. I shared the premises upon which I've built my career and consulting practice. First among those was my basic prescription for what organizations need to cure their ailments: honest conversations lead to thoughtful actions and improved performance.

Next, we looked at the curious phenomenon of Ought-But-Not Leaders. These are bright, well-trained individuals who know what elements contribute to success, but for a variety of reasons can't seem to implement those principles. We examined the possible sources of that internal resistance and suggested some ways that they might break through and realize their potential.

Ought-But-Not Leadership is all about passive resistance to doing the right thing. Now let's look at some active threats to organizational health, team performance, and constructive collaboration. Of course, this isn't an exhaustive list of all the possible threats that can impact a working culture, and your organization may be threatened by some problems we can't look at here. But in general, these are some common threats to success that I see on a daily basis in organizations that I work with. Honestly naming and understanding them is the first step to overcoming them. It will take honest conversations about the problems your team faces to move toward thoughtful actions to neutralize these threats and unleash your team's potential.

1. Misaligned Ego Is a Threat to Your Team

We all have an ego. The Merriam-Webster dictionary defines ego as "the opinion that you have about yourself." This means that to be conscious, to be alive, is to have an ego. That self-assessment might be accurate or wildly misaligned with reality. It might oversell your capabilities or grossly undersell your value. It might make it easier to work or live with you or much harder. But you have an ego, and you need to understand and channel it positively, or you will be working against it for the rest of your life.

When it comes to performing on the job and working in teams, the ego can be a powerful voice in our head. Hopefully, you hear it whispering positive and helpful statements:

- *"I am confident because I have done this before."*
- *"I am capable of doing this work."*
- *"I need help because this culture is new for me."*
- *"I am likable."*
- *"I will win."*

Ego is most at risk when we are in the midst of disorienting change. When change is too much, too fast, our self-perception is challenged by the unfamiliar landscape. Anytime our ego is at odds with reality, we are vulnerable. The odds that we will fail at a critical moment increase rapidly. For some of us, that's all the time. But, over time, most people find some sort of equilibrium between their ego and reality. Our self-perception may not be perfectly aligned with the world around us, but it's close enough to allow us to function reasonably well. But when disorienting change comes along, many of us can't recalibrate our self-assessment with the new facts quickly enough, and we stumble. That's when ego becomes destructive for us and for our teams.

I make it a habit to see interesting people speak. It's a great way to observe a professional at work and learn a few things in the process. Several years ago, I attended a speech by Greg Mortenson, the author of Three Cups of Tea, and I left with an interesting piece of information. Greg was telling the story of the first time he met General David Petraeus, who had just read his book. The general quickly gave him a summary of his book in three bullet points. After reading the book, the general observed that the keys to success in Afghanistan consist of, "Listening more, respecting the people, and building relationships."

This book became required reading for Petraeus' staff and many other parts of the military and government. This is a great example of a leader who was able to step back from a difficult situation, reassess what he knew and did not know, and plot a different path. In his leadership role, Petraeus could learn something new, recalibrate to that reality, and adjust his ego accordingly.

However, as bright and capable as they were, both Petraeus and Mortenson were ironically derailed by ego-related mistakes. For Mortenson, it was not getting the help to run his business well as it grew, and publishing a good story that might not have been a true story. No one would argue the impact Mortenson had with his schools, yet ego undermined the foundational story from his book and how he ran his growing organization.

For Petraeus, it was not his accomplishments as a general that were called into question, but his personal life. A destructive ego was involved somewhere in the decisions he made personally and his ability to openly own the consequences of those decisions.

Ego in leadership means recalibrating your self-perception based on new ideas and data from inside and outside your team. It is allowing others to lead through direct access to customers, other departments, and maybe even higher level leaders within an organization. It's the ability to honestly ask and answer questions like, "How am I doing? What do I need to change?" Technological change is testing this, because control is switching from being based on a hierarchy to more of a community. This means that information and decisions often flow around leaders, not through them. It could be creating a blog or an online community to bring people together around a common interest or goal. In these team situations, participation is voluntary. Healthy communities become bigger than the founder, and many people become leaders.

When a community grows, the ego can take different directions. It can stake out alternative positions:

- *"I started this and own it, so I will decide where it goes from here." (It's about me.)*
- *"I started this and am energized by its growth, and the voice of the community has to be part of where it goes from here." (It's not about me.)*

It is a decision point that is not unlike an employee stock ownership plan (ESOP), where a company gives ownership to the people who work there. This can be manipulated into a situation where the people get the ownership but do not have any voice, and as a consultant I have seen that happen and heard the frustrated voices of the people. It can also be managed where employees have legitimate ownership and feel the challenges of ownership in the decisions they have to make and the ups and downs of the market. They also feel the pride of ownership because of the voice they have in the community. A true community has many owners who are committed to one vision. But it does need a leader, and leading in that space will expose a destructive ego.

*Great leaders create movements by inspiring the
Tribe (i.e. Team) to communicate.*

Seth Godin

99

A great voice in this space is Seth Godin, who writes about this in his book Tribes. He observes that, "Great leaders create movements by inspiring the Tribe (i.e. Team) to communicate." Godin's challenge to lead in a tribe is very similar to the servant leadership idea that has been around for decades. While Godin is writing about a virtual community, it mirrors reasons Peter Drucker often shared that promoted leading in a not-for-profit situation as a development opportunity for any leader. Leading in situations where people have to want to follow you because they don't have to requires a leader to lead differently.

Ego allows us to make decisions quickly because of the confidence and experience that is attached to a healthy ego. It is the core of ego (i.e. the opinion we have of ourself) that made us stand out and brought us to a leadership role in the first place. New leaders quickly find themselves in situations where ego can be destructive, which is why this is the biggest threat to leaders and their ongoing success. It is not about whether we have an ego or not, but what form it takes as change happens.

2. Unbalanced Interaction Is a Threat to Your Team
It is not healthy to agree all the time. It is also not healthy to argue about everything. It is not about love or fighting, but about love and fighting. While ego is the number-one threat to a leader's effectiveness as an individual, the number-one threat to the relationships and effectiveness within a team is the wrong ratio between simple agreement (groupthink) and challenge (conflict).

I love the movie My Big Fat Greek Wedding. I'm from the Midwest, and several times I have been described as having a bad (good?) case of the "Midwest Nice." When I watched this movie, I marveled at how agape love and fighting could exist in the same family. As a husband, father, friend, business partner, and coach, I have continued to learn the lesson that love does not always mean total agreement.

John Gottman did some great research around this point in the area of marriage. He brought couples together and logged their interactions for fifteen minutes, tracking their positive and negative interactions. Using a ratio he developed, he was able to predict the success of that marriage with a 94% accuracy. The ratio was five positive interactions to one negative interaction. Relationships that went to one to one cascaded into divorce. Additional research also suggested that a ten to one ratio was equally as destructive. In other words, a healthy team finds a balance between groupthink and destructive conflict.

Would anyone argue that it is important to have a good balance of positive and negative interactions in a healthy relationship, whether it is a one-on-one or team? Probably not. All the great literature around teams and leadership from Drucker, Covey, Lencioni, and Collins has a part of the model devoted to difficult discussions (feedback) and celebrations (things we do well). The experts all talk about this threat within their models because it is the number-one threat to the effectiveness of a team and, if present, can make that team extremely effective. The line between threat and asset lies with your ability, as the leader, to model a style of listening to others, mining for conflict/ differing opinions, and to control your reactions so you are able to process what you hear before emotions drive your reactions.

You can take an assessment for yourself that will identify how you are most likely to respond to debate and where you are most likely to lead with emotion vs. rational thought. A foundational part of my coaching process is to do a personality profile assessment to test and build the self-knowledge of my clients and to give us a standard language to talk through challenges based on that self-knowledge.

While this is critical to my process, the reality for leaders, especially in smaller organizations, is that the resources and time to bring in an outside expert to help build this ability within you and your team are not always there. The place to start is with your abilities as the leader. One method I mentioned previously is to do a quick assessment of how many times a week people on your team disagree with you openly, and how often a solution to a problem comes from someone other than you. Take a couple days and keep notes on decision/discussions you have in your team meetings or when people approach you with a problem. Think of Gotman's ratio. Do you see a ratio favoring your team's ideas or your ideas? Do you see debate around problems, or just compliance with what you think? A heavily weighted ratio towards your opinion probably means the culture on your team supporting this debate is not there, and that people do not feel safe enough to argue? There is no fighting and love.

Know thyself. Listen for confusion or emotions that will distract from your ability to solve problems and work together. Those are the slow leaks of fear filling up the space in our heads that we need to use for thinking and reasoning to do our best work.

As opposed to the Ought-But-Not Leaders we talked about in the last chapter, great leaders ask great questions and listen for the answers. As I pointed out in the first chapter, great conversations start with an open-ended question. When it works, we have honest conversations that lead to thoughtful actions and improved performance. Over time, this will not allow fear to have a place inside your team by developing the habits that build a culture where love and fighting can coexist.

3. One-Size-Fits-All Motivation Is a Threat to Your Team

We think we are doing the right thing. The golden rule told us to treat others like we want to be treated. Noble, but wrong.

Roger Birkman discovered through his research that 70% of us have a communication style that is more direct that what our actual need for communication is. That means that I might be direct with you about what I am thinking, but any feedback you give me needs to be softened up or you risk hurting my feelings. That is true for 70% of people, and all it means is that a standard rule for balancing any criticism with some praise is a good habit. Going with a one-size-fits-all approach to how we treat people is very risky, and the Birkman research would say that is it the wrong approach.

Let's start with some background research on this topic. Frederick Herzberg did a study on motivation that he shared in his Harvard Business Review article "One More Time: How Do You Motivate Employees?" He found that the top four factors contributing to job satisfaction were achievement, recognition, work itself, and responsibility. Things like relationship with supervisor, salary, and work conditions only had an impact on performance if they were not present, and then they only contributed to job dissatisfaction.

During the most recent economic downturn, the Ken Blanchard Companies did a study to determine what people thought were the critical factors for a great work environment and who was responsible for each factor. The options for the second question were "myself," "my leader," and "senior leadership." The only two things given as overwhelming responsibilities (80% or more) to "my leader" were giving feedback and setting performance expectations. In addition, the respondents identified "myself" as having primary responsibility for connectedness with their leaders and colleagues. Kind words are nice, but it is getting the work done and getting feedback on that work that are the primary motivations of your best people.

In my opinion, we created this situation because of how we train new leaders and how we fail to remind them about the habits that make motivation personal. Motivation is routinely a topic in leadership training, and this section is focused on the question "What motivates people?" We use words like "recognition" and give them a script to make sure they know they are supposed to do it, and then they go off and lead with recognition and appreciation in their mind. What they find is multiple personalities on their teams, every day bringing different people issues they are dealing with, and their managers have forgotten the same recognition and appreciation training. The one thing they are sure about is what motivates them, and their picture of what motivates others becomes twisted based on what they hear on a day-to-day basis.

Here is an example of what I mean. I was doing a training on motivation with a group of seasoned leaders, and I started the conversation with two questions: "What are your top three motivators? What are the top three motivators for most of your team?" I used the Herzberg motivating factors list for them to choose from, and here are the answers:

Top three for me:

- *Achievement*
- *Responsibility*
- *Personal life (Recognition was #9)*

Top three for most of my team:

- *Salary*
- *Achievement*
- *Responsibility (Recognition was #5)*

In the debrief of the results, the reason given for salary being the top motivator was that it was the most common complaint they heard from their people, and the one problem they felt like they were always addressing. Herzberg would say recognition is second based on his research, yet this leadership group pushed it way down the list for themselves, and to fifth for their people.

I personally experienced this when the organization I was working for made a change to my responsibilities that expanded my team after only three months in a new role. My new leader brought me in, shared the change with me, and gave me a 3% raise because of the extra work they were going to ask of me. I left thankful for the money but hungry for more reasons for the change and knowledge of what the performance targets looked like in the new role. I did not give back the money, but I was clearly living in the Herzberg model, and my leader (who was in human resources) was following another list.

The first trap is to assume that everyone is motivated by the same thing. The second trap is to assume that people are motivated by what they talk about the most. In either case, understanding motivation requires that you:

a) Remember the basics and develop habits around those that will ensure you do not get too far off track.

b) Know your people. One size does not fit all, and allowing yourself to project your own motivators at the time to your people, or to react to what they are complaining about the most as their primary motivators, will always get you in trouble.

The leadership habits I will cover later center conversations around what is on their mind right now, knowing what their normal motivators are, and staying true to the foundational beliefs that certain things are strong motivators for most people, the top three being achievement, recognition, and the work itself. A good day is most always defined by being productive and liking what we do.

4. Stagnation Is a Threat to Your Team

What if you stopped learning in your job today, focusing instead on doing, being, and surviving instead of improving? How long would it take anyone to notice? If you are a leader, probably not very long, especially if your business is moving quickly and your team is being given new expectations. How many people on your team have stopped learning and looking for opportunities to grow? People who are not interested in getting better are a threat to great conversations and improved performance in your team.

When I worked in a manufacturing operation, we were always getting parts quoted at a price that made very little money on paper. However, we still did it because of the reputation of our technical leaders to make the necessary changes to the molding and assembly processes to improve the margins on the product so they were healthy. It was a risky strategy, but I saw it used successfully over and over again, and it provides a real example of the impact of a continuous improvement focus.

The opposite of leader is not follower; it's influencer.

Kate Nasser

99

Author and leadership blogger Kate Nassar put it this way: "The opposite of leader is not follower; it's influencer." Your so-called "followers" should ideally not be passive yes-men, but active players who have an influence on your team's direction. Influencers would abound if everyone saw themselves as a leader in their own role. Alas, that is not the case in the real world. Earlier, I talked about my belief that there are always a mix of A, B, and C-players in an organization. The proof comes from Gallup. Their surveys identify that about 23% of your people are top performers (i.e. influencers), 33% are willing to be influenced, and 44% will do their job but don't want any more responsibility.

Kate Nassar makes a great point about "followers" exerting influence on their leader, and the term "followership" is becoming more popular because it points to the importance of knowing our strengths and remembering that we all follow someone. I built off of her point on influencers and research on engagement to define the five levels of followership:

- **Minimizer.** *An individual who consumes oxygen in the workplace. They are present, but getting things done is not a priority. They measure their contribution by getting just enough done to stay employed.*
- **Doer.** *Someone who does what they are asked to do consistently and with very little negative emotion. They are solid and very dependable. They measure their contribution by getting done what is asked of them by the deadline.*
- **Attractor.** *An individual who does their job with joy, attracting customers both inside and outside of their organization. They measure their contribution by the smiles they receive and the work they get done.*
- **Improver.** *They do the work presented and look for ways to improve efficiency. These individuals measure their contribution by the dollars/ time they save or the improvements they make in the lives of their customers.*

- **Influencer.** *Someone who sees opportunities to alter strategies or activities that will have a big impact on the direction of the organization* *and the work that is being done. They measure their contribution by the big things they get started and the opportunities they have to engage in work they consider to be significant.*

Your best will always get better. The top 23% are looking for more and will find a way to have a greater influence, and sometimes that is enough. The only risk they pose to your business is that you might possibly lose good people or customers in the process of them learning the hard way when it comes to building and maintaining great relationships. But the risk is more than offset by the benefits. Plus, the real threat to your ability to lead is the 33% that are just waiting to follow. They are unlikely to get better, and even if they do improve, it won't be fast enough.

5. Fear Is a Threat to Your Team
Connecting with your people at a deeper level requires trust. When trust is present, people are willing to tell the truth, regardless of how difficult the message is to deliver. Leaders must tell the truth to build trust with their team, and ideally, their team members will also tell them the truth and contribute to the building of trust.

However, that's not always the case. Employees don't have to tell the truth because they are not subject to the same level of accountability and responsibility as leaders. They can just as easily stay quiet when they have frustrations or issues. Because of this, while there is much a leader knows about an organization, the bigger the organization, the less they are likely to know.

One of the things I did when I got my first leadership role was to cultivate a relationship with an employee who was social and who knew things. She wasn't a gossip, but someone who others would come to with questions or frustrations. That information was important because those were data points for engagement and for assessing how effectively we were communicating as a leadership team. I trusted her, and she trusted me, so she told me what I needed to hear, not what I wanted to hear. Other employees did not trust me enough to knock on my door, which I also understood. Knowing that also made me continue to strive to create a safe environment so everyone in the organization had someone they could talk to. One of my biggest frustrations as a leader was being surprised when someone exited the organization for a better opportunity. Leaving for growth is good, and it was even better when they felt safe enough to tell us what decision they were weighing so we could talk about it. Safety should be celebrated.

Safety is most fragile at the beginning of a relationship, when people do not know each other. One of these times is when there is a leadership transition. Establishing trust so people will feel the safety needed to share the truth is critical. Here are the moves that ruin a leaders chance at success:

- *Their first act is to fire someone.*
- *Their first act is to ask people to change a bunch of things the team has been doing forever and that they consider to be right.*
- *Their first act is to evaluate all the staff and make decisions about who stays and who moves.*

Leaders cannot be successful without their team helping them accomplish the work. Even in the situation of major change, leaders need a few people on their teams who trust them, feel safe enough to tell them the truth, and who will confront the fear in others with a perspective based on hope and optimism. Remember that fear is only a short-term motivator, and once it settles into a team the energy to remove it becomes far greater. You cannot be extremely successful without the brains, eyes, hands, mouths, and ears of your team, because there are too many things happening in your business for you to handle all the details.

Fear is a powerful motivator. Fear clouds the ability to share what we feel, the ability to see the true intent behind others' actions, and the ability to discern or ask for the intent behind others' words. Establishing safety means always being focused on driving fear out of your relationships. When there is more fear than safety in your team, honest conversations cannot happen.

Conclusion

As I said in the introduction to this chapter, you might think of the Ought-But-Nots listed in the last chapter as passive resistance to success—a headwind or current keeping some leaders and teams from moving forward as easily as they should be able to based on their talent and training. The threats I detailed in this chapter are active resistance—boulders rolling down the hill onto a mountain road, or sinkholes that can open up beneath your feet. Both active and passive resistance has to be overcome.

But how can you proactively overcome these negative limits? By cultivating positive habits in yourself, your team, and your working culture. In the next chapter, we'll look at a few of the habits I've seen help many of the individuals and organizations I've worked with.

Big Ideas from Chapter 3

- *Leaders need to be aware of the active threats to the healthy culture of their team, because when ignored these will destroy the culture quickly.*
- *Knowing these threats and acknowledging them is the first and biggest step to managing them.*
- *Here are the active threats to a leader trying to build a healthy and high performing team:*
  1. *Misaligned Ego: Too much or too little*
  2. *Unbalanced Interaction: I compliment more often than I criticize*
  3. *One -Size-Fits-All Motivation: People are different*
  4. *Stagnation: If you aren't learning you're dying*
  5. *Fear: It makes fight or flight the two main responses to anything*

Make Your Action Plan

Question to ask yourself	Your answer
1. I see my team making important decisions with minimal or no support from me.	Yes/No
2. If you followed me around all day I compliment more than I criticize, and when I give negative feedback I do it effectively and quickly.	Yes/No
3. I can tell you right now the primary motivators of all my team and I actively manage them using that knowledge.	Yes/No
4. I have development goals for myself and I am making time to get the learning I need to develop.	Yes/No
5. Love > Fear on my team.	Yes/No

Any question that you answered "No" to needs to be addressed so it does not cause any more damage to your effectiveness as a leader. An advanced application of this is to pick someone you work with that you trust, and ask them to answer these for you as a way of gathering feedback.

In making your action plan, as yourself, "What would it take for me to move from "No" to "Yes?" Pick one question and fix it. When that is done fix the next one. Repeat weekly or monthly.

Chapter 4
Habits

Your beliefs become your thoughts,
Your thoughts become your words,
Your words become your actions,
Your actions become your habits,
Your habits become your values,
Your values become your destiny.
Gandhi

99

To know and not do is to not yet know.
Kurt Lewin

99

It takes courage to grow up and become who you really are.
e.e. cummings

99

The Ought-But-Nots listed in Chapter 2 are like headwinds (passive resistance that keeps some leaders and teams from moving forward as easily as they should), and the organizational threats we talked about in Chapter 3 are like boulders rolling down the hill onto a mountain road (active resistance you must avoid). So how can leaders and teams spend more of their time and energy performing and less avoiding problems and pitfalls?

The answer lies in cultivating positive and proactive habits. Innovation is great, but constant innovation under stress might be evidence of a reactive leadership style. There's a reason why pilots, firefighters, soldiers, and surgeons practice procedures and rehearse their responsibilities. It's so that when problems arise and they are under stress to perform, their responses are reflexive. They don't always have to make it up as they go in a crisis. Even more, if they cultivate the right habits in their role, there will be fewer crises to react to.

In my work as a consultant and coach, I've identified at least four habits that people-centered leaders cultivate. I'm not suggesting that these will prevent all problems or eliminate stress and the need to respond creatively. But I am certain that leaders with these habits face fewer headwinds and are more easily able to dodge whatever boulders roll down the hillside into their path. There's an old saying: "It's better to fix the roof when the sun is shining." In the same way, I strongly suggest that the time to build constructive relationships, recharge your creative energy, develop your best people, and ask the right questions is when your team is in a good place, not in the midst of a storm.

Habit 1: Build Constructive Relationships

"Relationship" is a noun. It is something people or entities have. The dictionary defines it as the way in which two or more people, groups, countries, etc., are connected; it is the way they talk to, behave toward, and deal with each other.

My point is that relationships are neutral constructs, neither good nor bad in themselves. Their quality or value is assigned to them, subjectively, by the participants. The problem is that because a relationship necessarily has more than one member, it can be evaluated very differently by the people involved. Your relationship with a co-worker might mean a lot to you, and you might consider it to be pretty good. But as most of us have discovered (painfully), love, friendship, or respect is not always reciprocated. It's a complicated process, so let's focus on two aspects of it for leaders: starting the relationship with a new team member (on-boarding a new employee) and maintaining it over time.

Hiring a new employee means beginning a new relationship with them, and integrating them into the existing relationships on your team. There should be a sequence of priorities in cultivating this new working relationship. I say "should be" because these don't always happen, and they aren't even conscious priorities for many leaders—but they ought to be. Leaders who read this and think, "I know that" but aren't doing it are the very Ought-But-Not Leaders we talked about in Chapter 2. The sequence of priorities in on-boarding ought to be:

- *Build trust*
- *Build focus*
- *Build confidence*
- *Build rhythm*

In my consulting practice, this sequence of priorities is a key element in the leadership model I call trUPerformance™. As a people-centered model, it recognizes that the performance of our team will rise and fall based on the qualities of the working relationships we develop. No matter how much talent, brains, ambition, and opportunity our team has, if we can't work together effectively, our whole will be less than the sum of our parts. In order to work together effectively, we must build trust, focus, confidence, and rhythm between us. That takes understanding and effort, which requires honest conversations.

Since these ought to be our priorities in on-boarding new team members, we need to differentiate it from the hiring decision, at least in our own minds. The typical interview process often focuses exclusively on the work, the ability to do the work, and the fit to the team. Those are important considerations, and I'm not suggesting that we change those. But I am saying that even if a new employee flies through all those gates with green lights, a constructive relationship doesn't automatically develop. After the interview process and the hiring decision, the on-boarding process needs to focus on the foundation of trUPerformance™, building trust.

The existence of trust does not necessarily mean they like one another, it means they understand one another.

Peter Drucker

Peter Drucker astutely pointed out that, "The existence of trust does not necessarily mean they like one another, it means they understand one another." I meet many people who mistakenly assume that trust, focus, confidence, and rhythm must also include friendship. But as Drucker points out, every day we trust people who we don't necessarily like, or even know: airline pilots, doctors, vendors, etc. In a simple example, the barista that gave me my coffee this morning and I don't necessarily like each other (or dislike each other, since we're strangers). But we understand each other, and what each of us expects from the relationship: I want my coffee prepared in such a way, he wants courtesy, payment—and if he did an exceptional job, a tip. It's a perfectly functioning relationship, but our window of interaction is pretty narrow. If we worked together, the requirements for understanding and trust would increase proportionally. But we don't need to become friends to have a perfectly productive working relationship.

On-boarding is the most critical time in a relationship. In fact, I have a rule for any new leader: no firing anyone on the team for the first three months. It is no way to start a relationship with a team, mainly because the "understand one another" phase hasn't happened yet.

If you lead a team, reflect for a moment on this question: "What is your primary conscious goal when you bring on a new team member?" I was timing at a swim meet for kids between the ages of eight and thirteen. What do you think my primary role was? Timing? Actually, it wasn't. Of course, it was critical that I did my job and kept and recorded the times accurately. But my primary role was encouragement and support. I was supposed to make sure they were in the right order for the next race and tell them what they did well during that race. It was easy, because my natural voice is to encourage. I have known that for a while, and in order to be more effective at using that voice, I have had to work on knowing when that voice is not the one that is needed.

Your primary role when a new person starts is to get them comfortable so their best self can show up and the team can benefit from it. The key to doing this is remembering that you are not a mind reader, so ask questions and listen well.

To have committed and focused followers, you need to focus on these four things:

1. *Get to know them, and help them to get to know you. This happens by asking many of the questions that are not allowed in the interviewing process.*
2. *Make their roles and goals crystal-clear.*
3. *Provide the tools they need to be successful.*
4. *Allow them space to do and learn more, supporting them in success and failure.*

We're all busy, tempted to look for shortcuts and simple solutions, and so all too often we try a one-size-fits-all style of leadership. We rationalize it by saying that we're only treating everyone fairly, but our team is made up of individuals. They don't have a universal set of buttons that can be pushed or levers that can be pulled to increase performance. To understand what will draw the best out of each person, we need to ask great questions that lead to honest conversations. In the on-boarding phase, great conversations means asking them lots of questions over the first few months on your team. For example:

- *"Tell me more about your family/what you do outside of work/other things that did not make it to your resume."*
- *"What are your preferred communication method(s)?"*
- *"When is it OK to interrupt you, and when is it not?"*
- *"How will I know whether you're stressed, irritated, or open to debate?"*
- *"What irritates you?"*

After you gather information about them, be open about answering the same questions. Don't try and read their minds, and don't expect them to be able to read yours. Your goal is to get the key information you will need to help them manage the fear of starting a new role.

Just like ego can get in the way of you leading, it can also get in the way of bringing in a person with experience who might not be used to being the "new person." We've all heard the cliche, "There is no 'I' in team." It's a great slogan, but it's wrong. Just like leaders, people have egos, and professionals usually have significant egos. Smart leaders look for people who have been successful somewhere else. Individually, this success happens because of their personal drives to succeed. That means there has to be room for "I" somewhere in their work. The brightest and best need an opportunity to shine. Your job as a leader is to find a way to let everyone on your team find a way to shine that satisfies their need for significance and professional success without detracting from the team effort. Part of on-boarding (and even the interview process) is having an open and honest conversation focused on defining both individual needs and team goals, then deciding if a balance can be achieved.

Accomplishing this balance starts with a series of conversations with potential team members to identify:

1. *A list of what they bring to the team, including strengths and weaknesses.*
2. *A list of things they want or need from the team.*
3. *A list of personal reasons for joining the team, including what they see as the group's goals or potential.*

If on-boarding is done well, two things happen. First, people become comfortable sooner because they get to know you as a person and as a leader, and that familiarity allows them to start seeing your behaviors as normal for you. Think back to the Drucker quote on trust: "they understand one another." The second part of doing on-boarding well comes when people demonstrate competence with their team members and you by being successful. I call these wins. Wins start to build trust with others because they provide a frame of reference for an important part of a peer relationship: I can count on them to get their piece of our collective work done.

Process these pieces by sharing openly, identifying common themes in both individual needs and team goals. Challenge people to identify needs that are purely "Me" goals (e.g. keeping one's top twenty clients) and those that are "We" goals that benefit the entire team (e.g. offering a more complete service solution to customers). By systematically going through these conversations, it will become evident whether or not potential team members are compatible, and whether joining the team is the right move for an individual.

On-boarding is focused on building trust, with the outcome being foundational understanding of what usual behaviors are, and when stress is happening. Then life happens. Business happens. Change happens. Natural shifts happen, and the usual and normal that we established with job priorities and life priorities need to be reexamined and sometimes reset. The only way to do that is through ongoing honest conversations. There are two critical conversation that will help keep your relationship with your people on track and help you move from OUGHT TO to DO in your commitment to lead them by involving them: one-on-one meetings and performance evaluations.

I remember the moment I became passionate about one-on-ones and performance conversations. I was in the midst of my second day supporting a nationally known author/consultant in the area of conflict management/robust conversations. My organization was sixteen months into a curriculum rollout/organizational change, and the success was present, but only in pockets. While the curriculum he provided was excellent, it was not providing the outcomes we expected. As we went from group to group getting feedback on successes and failures, a question came to my mind, so I asked it. "Bill, in your assumptions of organizations and relationships between leaders and their teams, do you assume that leaders are meeting one-on-one with their teams regularly?" His answer: "Yes." It hit me that we can equip leaders all day long to have these wonderful, fierce, crucial, or honest conversations, and yet if they are not creating controlled space that is safe and focused (like a one-on-one conversation), it will be difficult to practice and change habits. More importantly, the failure rate must not exceed the success rate. Failure in the area of building relationships (i.e. leadership) is expensive at many levels.

That is also when I realized that I would start a crusade around habits that mean the most to people (i.e. engagement), and that busy leaders, if they are willing to practice them, will get the biggest ROT (return on time).

Great feedback is the secret to personal growth. Growth can happen without it, but if it is just based on what we think, it falls into the "We think we are getting better, but we aren't" category.

I made this same point while facilitating a class. At the next break, one of the participants came up to me and asked for feedback based on my interactions with them. I applaud their willingness to seek feedback, but it was the wrong place to start because there was no context. Some feedback is too broad. If you want feedback, you need some structure, or even tools, for creating a safe environment and getting valuable feedback. I have some great tools available on my website: *www.thetrugroup.com/resources/talent-management-templates/.*

Habit 2: Regularly Reset, Realign, and Recharge

I had the opportunity to share a cup of coffee with two very successful leaders, one a CEO/entrepreneur and the other a senior pastor. As they shared their challenges, a common point emerged: "Leaders have to make decisions and live with the results." As we talked about what "living with" the results meant in practical terms, one key point emerged: leadership can be lonely.

In another conversation with a leader, they shared with me a similar concern. "I feel like I'm constantly reacting as a leader and spending most of my time dealing with the daily work instead of looking ahead and planning," he said. "I'm tired, and I feel like my people are getting burned out."

Let's think back to our chapters on Ought-But-Not Leaders and organizational threats. Whether it is a feeling of loneliness or burnout, the foundation is that we are not getting to the things that replenish our energy reserves. In our "ought to" language, we are allowing our priorities to be dictated by others. In "threat" language, our ego is getting in the way of asking for help or handing things off to others.

It would take less than sixty seconds of searching on Google or Bing to come up with credible evidence linking stress with health issues. There are things we can do to manage this, but we first have to address the very things that are getting in the way. Who reading these pages has the following life goals?

- *I plan on working extremely hard, eating whatever I want, avoiding exercise, and dealing with my Type 2 Diabetes and/or heart disease when and if it happens.*
- *I am willing to sacrifice key relationships in my life for the career I want. A healthy marriage and close friends would be nice, but they are not my priorities.*

There are some certainties if you are a leader. Each day and week you will be faced with big decisions that could have a huge impact on the organization. When you do make a decision, the feedback often gets personal: people objecting to or arguing the decision. There will be personal attacks on the leader (you) by people outside of the decision-making loop. (Ask a pastor about this one!)

Gallup did a study that found people who had three close friends at work were 96% more likely to be extremely satisfied with their lives. I never read in their results the caveat, "except for CEOs or executives." You may feel different, but you are not.

Leadership sages Stephen Covey and Peter Drucker both shared the same advice with leaders around self-care. Covey talked about sharpening the saw, which is a time of reflection and self-renewal that rejuvenates us so we can return to our work and life with new energy and renewed focus. Drucker shares the concept of feedback analysis, which is a continuous loop of personal feedback to set goals, do the work, and revisit the work to constantly hone your own knowledge of where you are at your best.

In order to be able to reset and recharge, most leaders need to know that the team is functional enough for them to temporarily disengage. They can't do that if they aren't dialed into what's going on. The leader who wants to be able to disengage in order to reset and realign has to be able to accurately assess the status quo, which means they have to be able to listen and grasp what's going on inside and around the leader. Here are a few tips to do that:

- **Observe.** *What is your energy level coming to work? Do you see your people taking initiative, or do you have to repeat things many times or do them yourself? What is your energy level when you leave? Take five minutes to answer these questions three times a week for the next two weeks. What does it tell you?*

- *Ask people.* *How are your people feeling about things? For an organization with fewer than seventy-five people, schedule some breakfasts and start the conversation with questions like: "What's working? What should we start doing? What should we stop doing? What are you wondering about?" Ask and listen. This also gives you a chance to share some of the things that are keeping you up at night, with the goal of finding some solutions to the problems you face.*

Both these actions will help you identify things in your own work and your organization that are working, and things that are broken. It is a key in every conversation to identify what is working, because that will provide little boosts of energy for yourself and your organization. Progress and getting work done leads to renewed energy. Jim Collins calls this the Flywheel Effect in his classic book, Good to Great. In his study of successful companies, Collins discovered that they all did a great job defining the big goals, understanding the work that needed to be done to achieve the goals, and celebrating as the work was completed. The flywheel is a symbol for the business making progress, and as it turns it develops momentum for the business. It becomes easier to turn with every successful rotation. We gain energy from successes.

It is important for you to listen to yourself and your business, but it is also important to develop a circle of people around you who can provide needed empathy, support, and ideas for your work. Here are three ways to accomplish that:

- *Get a small network (three to five people) of peers: Part of my work is with second-stage growth companies, which are smaller companies entering a stage of growth where the business is getting bigger than what the leader can manage on his/her own. My job is to help the leader increase his or her capacity to lead and to develop a team around them that will share the work of leadership. As part of my* work, I always encourage a leader to find a peer group where they can be with people who are on the same journey. Peer groups provide a safe place to share ideas and frustrations, get advice, and be reminded that others have bigger problems than you. Safety was presented earlier as a real threat to leaders getting feedback and ideas from their people. It is also a barrier for you when you look inside your company for a place to be yourself. While you need to be transparent with your team, if you are a CEO, this network should be outside the organization.

- **Become an expert at:**
    a. Finding a positive outlet for stress (it is part of your job and it is not going away).
    b. Taking time twice a year (in addition to your vacations) to get away from the office to recalibrate your personal and professional priorities and to reenergize. Sharpening the saw and self-reflection are not urgent tasks, but they are important. I know a CEO who has actually found a peer group that takes him away from the office each quarter for a couple of days, and he uses that time to find support for his work and get some time to recharge.

- **Make sure your team is practicing the same principles.**
    Do you really want your executive team making decisions from a place of loneliness, fear, or insecurity? Will your newly-hired VP be more productive if s/he is feeling lonely or s/he has one or two friends to openly share frustrations with or get advice from? When you adopt habits for a healthier self, getting your leadership team involved will create a support network around you. I know of teams that always schedule some exercise together during their off-sites or engage in fitness challenges once or twice a year. This third habit will reinforce your focus in number two and increase your chance for overall success.

One reason executive coaching has taken off in the last decade is because the pace of business has changed significantly. Making a personal change is a challenge, and now it's even harder because there's so much to do on a day-to-day basis. One big question that sums up this habit of reset and recharge is, "Are things where they need to be for me personally and for my business?" Within the answer has to be a compelling "why" for making a change. The role of a coach mirrors that of a peer group in a couple of ways. First, the coaching relationship is a safe place to process things that need to be talked about, whether they are frustrations or possible solutions to a problem. Secondly, it provides both support and accountability for the leader, which are the two critical ingredients for making a successful personal shift or change. In this way, a coach becomes a key partner and sounding board in the work, and will help make the changes stick.

Habit 3: Deliberately Develop Your Best People

Ought-But-Not Leaders get frustrated by time—there's never enough of it for them, it passes by them inconsistently, and they can't figure out how to use it effectively. My response to their frustration is to pivot them from blaming time to realizing how much of their work they allow to be dictated by others. It is a reality that leaders are just like anyone else: they have twenty-four hours in a day, and there is nothing they can do to add an hour. It is also critical to recognize that there will be lots of interruptions in a leader's day, especially those that lead smaller organizations. By the way, 99.9% of organizations have less than five hundred people, and they employ roughly 46% of all people that are working. My recommendation to leaders is focus your limited resources and time towards your best people. An overall threat to your organization is that not enough people are getting better, and it is important to remember what motivates your best people. In his book What Got You Here Won't Get You There, Marshall Goldsmith asked two hundred "high potentials" (junior leaders identified as having qualities that could take them to the top) the question, "If you stay in this company, why are you going to stay?" The three top answers were:

- *"I am finding meaning and happiness now. The work is exciting and I love what I am doing."*
- *"I like the people. They are my friends. This feels like a team. It feels like a family. I could make more money working with other people, but I don't want to leave the people here."*
- *"I can follow my dreams. This organization is giving me a chance to do what I really want to do in life."*

Creating a development plan for each of your best people solidifies a relationship with them and gets them involved in exciting work. Back to our definition of relationship, it is establishing a new connection with them. By identifying them, we are also creating a new way we relate to each other: leader to leader.

The true expense of developing your future leaders will impact your time, your most valuable resource. You will need to spend time selecting, mentoring, teaching, and providing feedback to your future leaders. Building a program with limited resources means having a rigorous selection conversation, committing time to spend with the participants, and fostering ownership and community within your future leaders.

Here is an outline of the steps you can take to start developing your next generation of leaders:

1. **Selection:** *With your leadership team, brainstorm a list of characteristics you look for in a leader, ultimately settling on the five to seven most important items. Next, create a list of people in your*

*organization whom you believe would make good leaders. Include
both those expressing interest in leadership and those identified by the
leadership team. Finally, evaluate each candidate based on your criteria
and pick the top five to ten.*

2. **Create a Community:** *Bring the group of leadership candidates
together monthly for check-ins, group activities, and learning from senior
executives.*

3. **Assign a Mentor:** *Assign a mentor—a current leader within the
company—to each future leader. Future leaders should meet monthly
with their mentors. In a smaller organization, the role of the leader is
the mentor.*

4. **Focus All Learning Provided to This Group on Three Areas:**

   a. **Build Self-Knowledge:** *Back to the same point made earlier by
   Aristotle, "know thyself." Use the Harvard Business Review article
   "Managing Oneself" by Peter Drucker to structure the conversation.
   Have the leadership candidates read and answer all of the questions
   presented in the article and review the results with their mentors*

   b. **Lead:** *Each future leader should seek out two opportunities to
   lead something—one within the organization and one outside, such
   as volunteering, not-for-profit work, coaching, etc. Mentors and
   candidates should review these leadership experiences to expand
   self-understanding, discuss what was learned, and identify future
   development needs.*

   c. **Communication:** *All leaders have to be great communicators.
   The most effective way to accomplish this is by making a
   commitment to attend Toastmasters for one year. This is an area
   that has to be practiced. While there are one and two day classes*

that help, the best and most cost-effective way to improve in this area is joining Toastmasters. In addition, look for opportunities to put this person in front of groups. When you do full-company meetings, give these individuals a chance to talk in front of people.

Follow up your leadership development program by:

1. *Finding ways for each of your current leaders to spend time with each candidate throughout the year.*
2. *Repeating the yearly conversation to review and revise the list of candidates. Your time is the most valuable currency you can use to show your future leaders they are valued. Invest well.*

Habit 4: Ask (and Answer) Powerful Questions

Great conversations start with a question. In my experience, where leaders tend to get into trouble is when they stop listening and focusing a portion of their actions on what they hear. The great leaders I have had the pleasure to know and observe consistently do a couple of things that cultivate great conversations:

- *They set up times to interact with people at all levels of their organization to just listen to their people's priorities and get their opinion on things.*
- *They keep a couple of powerful questions ready for conversations with leaders, peers, and other interesting people they meet.*

Another lens you can look at questions through is the organizational threats that keep you from leading with the priorities of relationships and trust. Revisit Chapter 3 for more discussion of organizational threats. For our purpose here, let's consider the ego threat. Great questions make our ego step back and give space for others. Imagine a situation where you have ten-plus years of experience in an area you are leading, and one of your team has a problem. Ask questions like, "What do you see as the main issues? Based on your experience and knowledge, what options are there? Which one would you chose and why?" Your less-experienced team members might not come up with the right answer (or the same answer you would have, which is not necessarily the same thing!), but they will probably get close, which gives you a chance to affirm the part of their answer that is closest to the truth and help them think through the rest of a pretty solid solution.

Great questions have the ability to continue a conversation where we are disagreeing with others, and provide a space for the opinions of others to have value (love). Imagine a heated argument where you walked in with a plan and it is not being well received by others. You might say, "I came in here today ready to go and thinking this plan was refined and ready, and I am sensing that it would be good to step back and rethink a few things. Would you be willing to spend a little time reviewing some of the key pieces and give me some of your thoughts and feedback?" That changes the dynamic in the team, and puts it onto a more collaborative path.

Great questions will reveal the motivations of others. One tip I always give leaders when they are doing breakfasts or question/answer sessions with people is to start by having everyone ask one question they have or someone on their team has asked (this option makes it safer!). By writing those questions down, you will get a sense of what people care about at that moment. How is the company performing? How will our benefits be impacted by the recent changes to healthcare by Congress? Why did we stop having an employee picnic?

Making time for questions to be asked and answered shows a commitment to safety and sharing. Ultimately, whether a person feels safe to answer is their choice, but by asking questions routinely, listening to answers, and following up in some way—even if it is a sincere, "No"—we create conditions where people have a much better chance of feeling safe.

Here are some of the questions I have offered during my trUTips. Read them, edit them, and in the end find a couple that you really like and USE them.

Questions to start your week as a WILL DO vs. Ought-But-Not Leader:

- *"How am I going to hand out praise today?"*
- *"Who is going to get it? "*
- *"Who do I need to check in with?"*
- *"Who do I seem to be missing lately that I need to find?"*
- *"Have I sat down, one-on-one, and talked with them about their performance and what they need in the last sixty days?"*

Check-in questions with your people:

- *"What wins did you have this week?"*
- *"What is your number-one frustration right now?"*
- *"What support do you need to have a great rest of the week? Month? Year?"*

Self-reflection:

- *"What are the five characteristics/skills you feel are important for leaders to possess at your organization?"*
- *"Which of these are strengths for me?"*
- *"Which one do I need to focus on getting better at?"*

- *"Who can help me?"*

Five levels of leadership (Collins):
1 *Highly Capable Individual*
2 *Contributing Team Member*
3 *Competent Manager*
4 *Effective Leader*
5 *Level-Five Executive*
   - *"How would I rate myself?"*
   - *"How would my leader rate me?"*
   - *"How would my people rate me?"*

Five levels of followership (Patchin):
1 *Minimizer*
2 *Doer*
3 *Attractor*
4 *Improver*
5 *Influencer*
   - *"How would I rate myself?"*
   - *"How would my leader rate me?"*
   - *"How would my people rate me?"*

Think about your very best people, and ask:
- *"Have I given him/her a compliment in the last month?"*
- *"Has s/he gotten a meaningful reward in the last year?"*
- *"What is the development plan for this person?"*
- *"What is the future spot in the organization that matches his/her career goals?"*

What are the most critical roles in my organization?

- *"Of the people in these roles, who would I hire again?"*
- *"Who would I not hire?"*
- *"What is my plan for the people who I would not hire again?"*
- *"Do I have a list of people I could move into these roles if someone left?"*

Questions that hand ownership back to your people:

- *"What solutions have you considered?"*
- *"Which solution would you recommend?"*
- *"How can I support you?*

Big Ideas from Chapter 4

- *The secret to overcoming the passive and active threats that derail leaders is to cultivate positive and proactive habits.*
- *Habits happen when we rehearse and practice them.*
- *The key habits that people-centered leaders practice and master are:*

   1. *Build constructive relationships. Few people die wishing they had more stuff. Many die wishing that they had more friends.*

   2. *Regularly reset, realign, and recharge. Your state of mind will influence how you lead. This ensures you lead from a healthy place.*

   3. *Be deliberate about developing your best people. It will have the biggest impact on your most valuable resource, your time.*

   4. *Ask (and answer) powerful questions. Great questions make us think and push us to get better and smarter.*

Make Your Action Plan

Question to ask yourself	Your answer
1. If I look at my calendar for last week, I see at least two activities at work and two activities at home where I am focused on building relationships.	Yes/No
2. I set aside at least an hour each week to shut out the world and spend time reviewing my priorities, doing or dumping the things I am procrastinating on, and thinking about how my team is performing and what I need to be doing to help support them and move us towards our goals.	Yes/No
3. I have a list of my best performers and I have checked in with each of them in the last quarter about their development and have each on a key project.	Yes/No
4. In the last week I can point to two meetings where I coached my team using powerful questions that resulted in them coming up with some great action plans without my input.	Yes/No

Any question that you answered "No" to needs to be addressed so it does not cause any more damage to your effectiveness as a leader. An advanced application of this is to pick someone you work with that you trust, and ask them to answer these for you as a way of gathering feedback.

In making your action plan, as yourself, "What would it take for me to move from "No" to "Yes?" Pick one question and fix it. When that is done fix the next one. Repeat weekly or monthly.

Conclusion

I have no illusion that reading this book has changed your life, but I do hope that it gave you a few "Aha!" moments. Of course, what's interesting and wonderful is that those moments will have been different for each reader. We are, after all, individuals. We come from different places, and we're at different points along our leadership journey. But we all have, I hope, the same destination in mind: we want to perform better, as individuals and with our teams. At various moments in our career this or that insight—or even an offhand comment—might be just what we need to help us make sense out of whatever we're dealing with, or inspire us to action.

Which brings me to action. We can consume a lot of leadership books and conferences and gain much wisdom, but it's not useful unless we put it to use. I hope that you did more than just exclaim, "Aha!" at some point in this book; I hope that you got up out of your chair or left your office and went out and did something. Perhaps it was to start an honest conversation by asking a great question. That would be great place to start. Remember, as I said at the beginning,

Honest conversations lead to thoughtful actions and improved performance.
99

It's possible, even probable, that not only did you gain new insight into yourself, but you had an "Aha!" moment about someone else, someone you work with. For example, perhaps you realized that your boss is an Ought-But-Not Leader. What do you do about that? You can't change someone else, right?

Right. You can't change someone else. But you can, and do, own the choice of what to do about it. What conversation needs to happen? Is it an honest conversation with your boss or teammate to address an issue that is holding back your team's performance? Make the choice to have an honest conversation. ...The journey continues on the next page.

Blessings,

Scott

So where does the journey go from here?

I wrote this book to invite leaders into an introspective journey about how effective they were at leading with a people-centered approach. By now you have thought about your beliefs and examined some of the things that might be derailing your actions and causing your intent to get lost. If I am honest with myself, I often find myself becoming the Ought-But-Not Leader that I am trying to avoid. When that happens, I work really hard to not stay there, and to say I am sorry to the people that deserve a better me.

Now it is time to go to work, because the internal work you have done is great, now the world needs to experience it and it starts with getting you and your team on the Honest Culture Journey™. On the next page is how I experience it personally and in my work as an EOS (Entrepreneurial Operating System) Implementer.™ I have watched leaders and their teams live it and I have watched them suffer because they are just not able to follow this path. My next book is designed to unpack this journey for each of you and equip you with some simple things you can do to experience it in your life and in your team.

Honest Culture Journey™

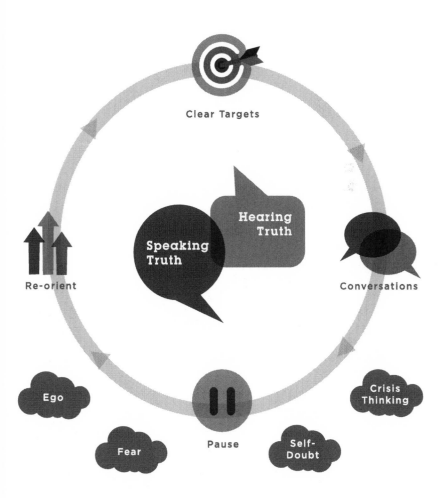

Action Plan Workspace

Action Plan Workspace

Action Plan Workspace